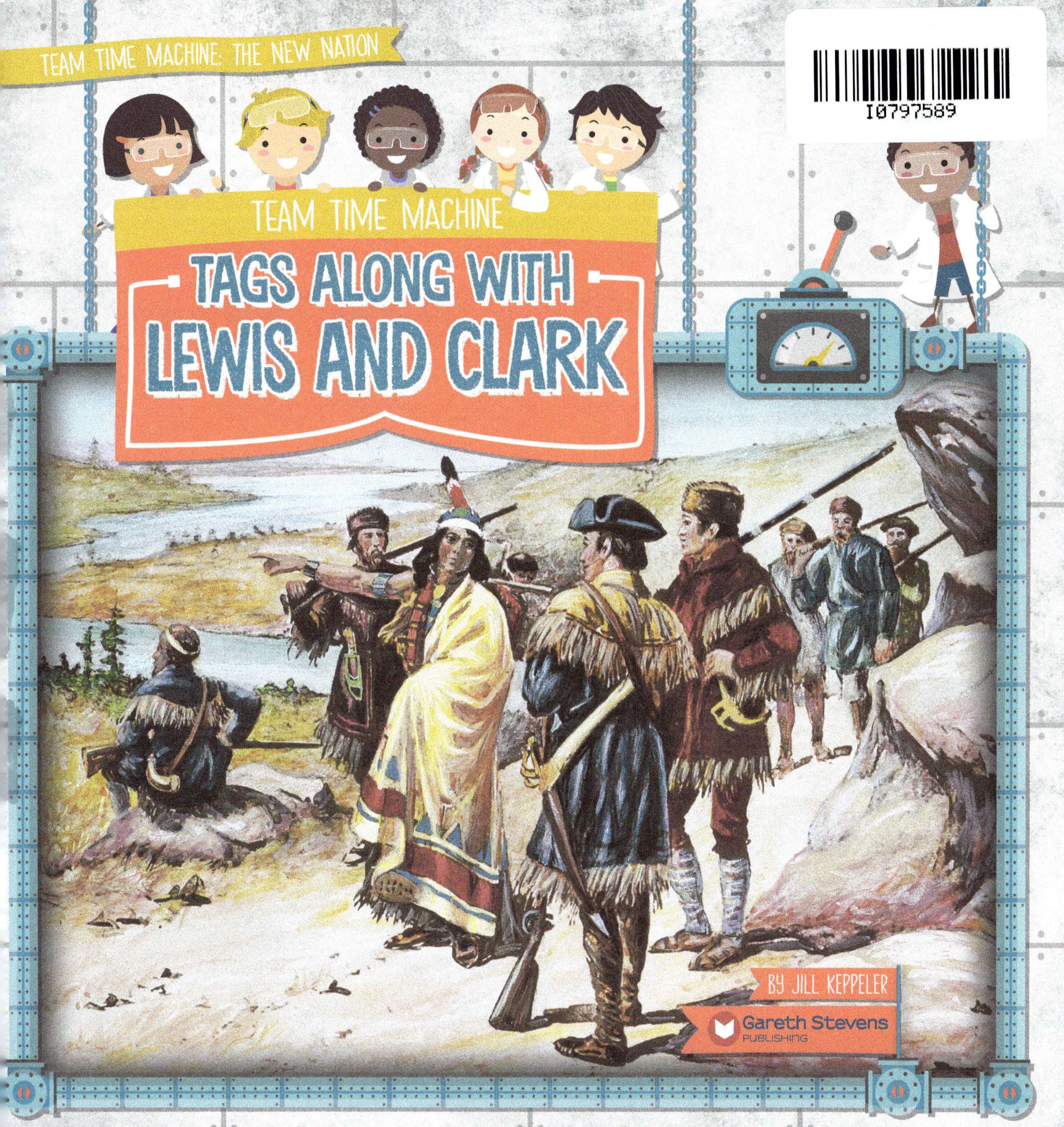
TEAM TIME MACHINE: THE NEW NATION
I0797589
TEAM TIME MACHINE
TAGS ALONG WITH
LEWIS AND CLARK
BY JILL KEPPELER
Gareth Stevens
PUBLISHING

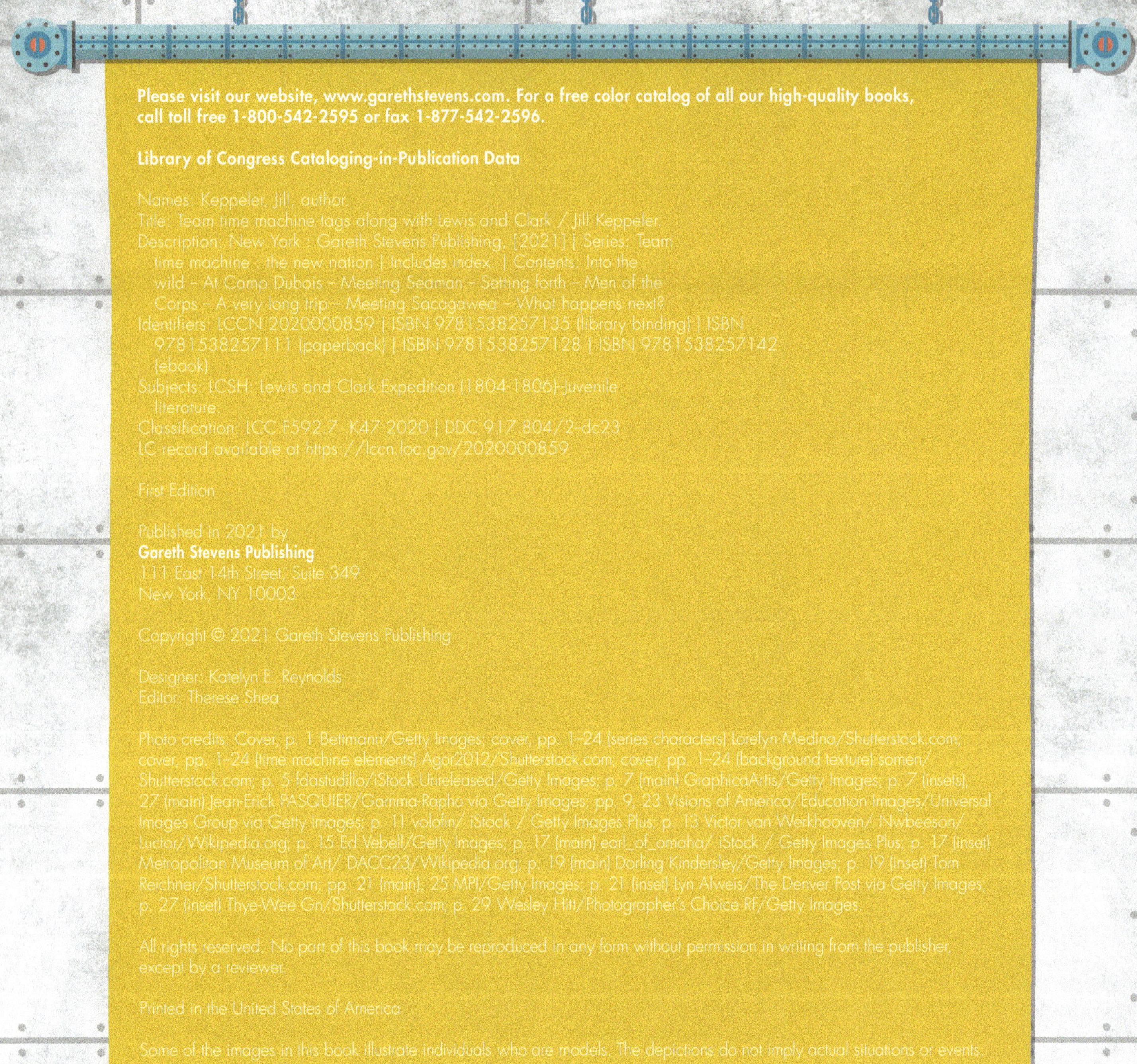

Please visit our website, www.garethstevens.com. For a free color catalog of all our high-quality books, call toll free 1-800-542-2595 or fax 1-877-542-2596.

Library of Congress Cataloging-in-Publication Data

Names: Keppeler, Jill, author.
Title: Team time machine tags along with Lewis and Clark / Jill Keppeler.
Description: New York : Gareth Stevens Publishing, [2021] | Series: Team time machine : the new nation | Includes index. | Contents: Into the wild – At Camp Dubois – Meeting Seaman – Setting forth – Men of the Corps – A very long trip – Meeting Sacagawea – What happens next?
Identifiers: LCCN 2020000859 | ISBN 9781538257135 (library binding) | ISBN 9781538257111 (paperback) | ISBN 9781538257128 | ISBN 9781538257142 (ebook)
Subjects: LCSH: Lewis and Clark Expedition (1804-1806)–Juvenile literature.
Classification: LCC F592.7 .K47 2020 | DDC 917.804/2–dc23
LC record available at https://lccn.loc.gov/2020000859

First Edition

Published in 2021 by
Gareth Stevens Publishing
111 East 14th Street, Suite 349
New York, NY 10003

Designer: Katelyn E. Reynolds
Editor: Therese Shea

Photo credits: Cover, p. 1 Bettmann/Getty Images; cover, pp. 1–24 (series characters) Lorelyn Medina/Shutterstock.com; cover, pp. 1–24 (time machine elements) Agor2012/Shutterstock.com; cover, pp. 1–24 (background texture) somen/Shutterstock.com; p. 5 fdastudillo/iStock Unreleased/Getty Images; p. 7 (main) GraphicaArtis/Getty Images; p. 7 (insets), 27 (main) Jean-Erick PASQUIER/Gamma-Rapho via Getty Images; pp. 9, 23 Visions of America/Education Images/Universal Images Group via Getty Images; p. 11 volofin/ iStock / Getty Images Plus; p. 13 Victor van Werkhooven/ Nwbeeson/ Luctor/Wikipedia.org; p. 15 Ed Vebell/Getty Images; p. 17 (main) earl_of_omaha/ iStock / Getty Images Plus; p. 17 (inset) Metropolitan Museum of Art/ DACC23/Wikipedia.org; p. 19 (main) Dorling Kindersley/Getty Images; p. 19 (inset) Tom Reichner/Shutterstock.com; pp. 21 (main), 25 MPI/Getty Images; p. 21 (inset) Lyn Alweis/The Denver Post via Getty Images; p. 27 (inset) Thye-Wee Gn/Shutterstock.com; p. 29 Wesley Hitt/Photographer's Choice RF/Getty Images.

Printed in the United States of America

Some of the images in this book illustrate individuals who are models. The depictions do not imply actual situations or events.

CPSIA compliance information: Batch #CS20GS: For further information contact Gareth Stevens, New York, New York at 1-800-542-2595.

CONTENTS

WORDS IN THE GLOSSARY APPEAR IN **BOLD** TYPE THE FIRST TIME THEY ARE USED IN THE TEXT.

CHAPTER 1: INTO THE WILD

"You've looked sad all day. What's wrong?" Mia asked her friend Ben. She sat down next to him in the lunchroom. Their friend Sam sat on Ben's other side.

Ben sighed. "I was supposed to go camping with my uncle next weekend," he said, looking down at his lunch. "But now he has to work. He can't go."

Mia and Sam glanced at each other.

"I have an idea," Mia said. "Do you remember what we were talking about in history class today?"

MEET TEAM TIME MACHINE

TEAM TIME MACHINE IS A GROUP OF FRIENDS WHO FOUND A TIME MACHINE ONE DAY IN A VERY ODD LIBRARY. THEY DISCOVERED THAT BOOKS FROM THE LIBRARY COULD POWER THE MACHINE AND TRANSPORT THEM TO DIFFERENT PLACES AND TIMES. IN THIS ADVENTURE, BEN, MIA, AND SAM GO ON A TRIP WITH THE FAMOUS **EXPLORERS** LEWIS AND CLARK!

TODAY, YOU CAN VISIT LEWIS AND CLARK HISTORICAL PARKS IN THE STATES OF WASHINGTON AND OREGON.

Ben looked up at her, eyes widening. "You mean the Lewis and Clark **expedition**?" He lowered his voice. He only wanted his friends to hear. "You want to use the library to go camping in 1803?"

Mia smiled. "Why not? We'd learn a lot and be back before math class!"

The three friends hurried to the library. Sam found a book on the travels of Lewis and Clark, put it in the time machine, and pulled the handle. The room spun and shook as the kids went back in time!

IN MAY 1803, THE UNITED STATES BOUGHT FRENCH TERRITORY IN NORTH AMERICA. THIS WAS CALLED THE LOUISIANA PURCHASE. MERIWETHER LEWIS, WILLIAM CLARK, AND OTHERS EXPLORED PART OF THIS AREA. THEIR TEAM WAS CALLED THE **CORPS** OF DISCOVERY.

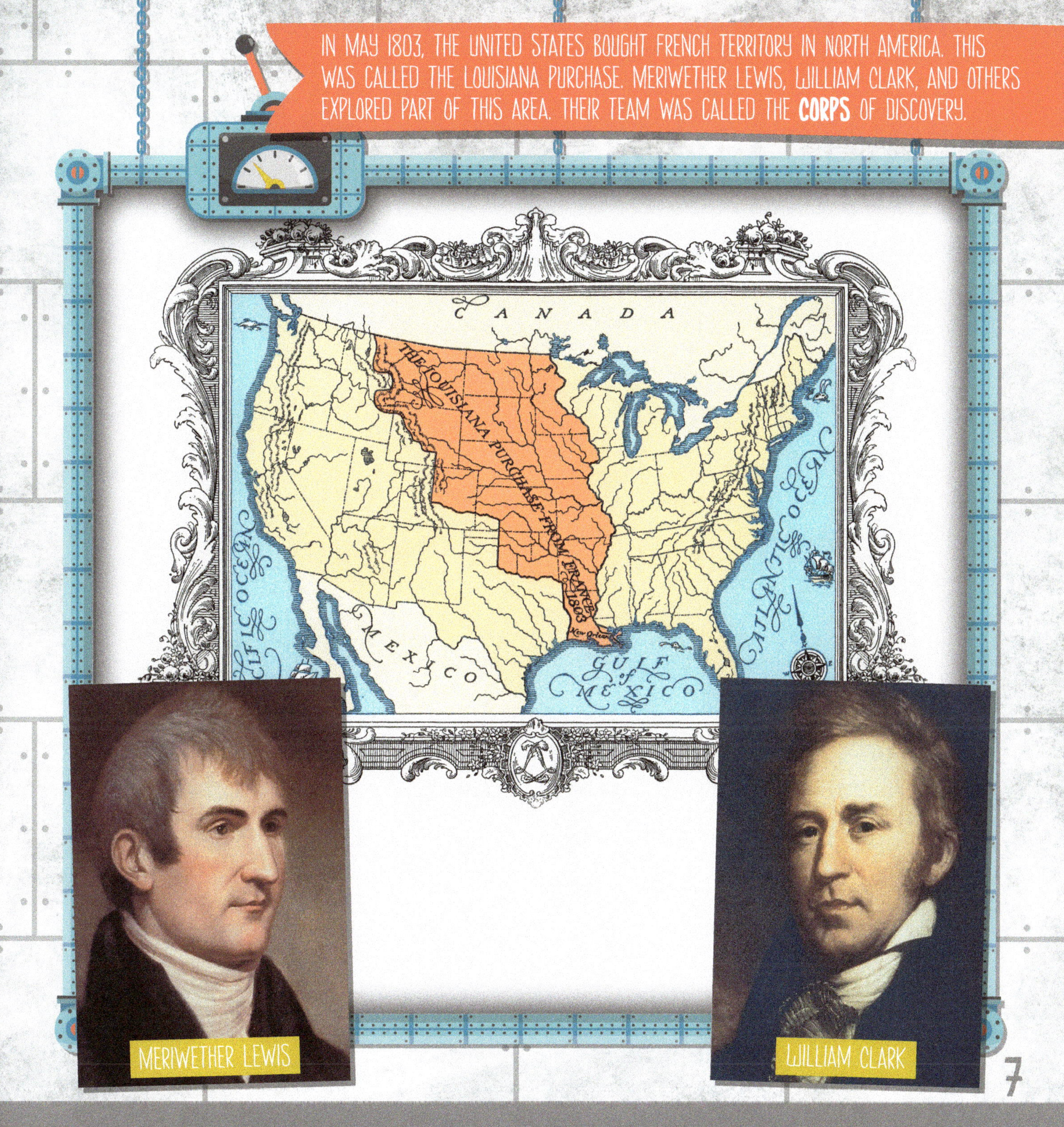

MERIWETHER LEWIS

WILLIAM CLARK

CHAPTER 2: AT CAMP DUBOIS

Sam peeked out the door of the library, which now looked like a log cabin. "I think it's Camp Dubois! That's where the Corps of Discovery left from on May 14, 1804."

Mia and Ben looked out. There were men moving around, and they could hear voices.

"I think they're getting ready to leave," Mia said. "We need to hurry!"

A bag was sitting outside the door. It held extra clothes for the travelers. They put some on to fit in better. Sam left the library first. Suddenly, Mia and Ben heard him yell!

THE ORIGINAL CAMP DUBOIS IS PROBABLY UNDERWATER SINCE THE MISSISSIPPI RIVER HAS SHIFTED, OR MOVED, SINCE THEN.

TODAY, A **RE-CREATION** OF CAMP DUBOIS STANDS IN THE LEWIS AND CLARK STATE HISTORIC SITE. IT'S ON THE MISSISSIPPI RIVER, NORTH OF ST. LOUIS, MISSOURI.

CHAPTER 3: MEETING SEAMAN

Worried, Ben and Mia ran after Sam. They found him right outside, staring at a big, black, furry creature that was staring back at him.

"It's a bear!" Sam shouted. "There's a bear in the camp!"

Mia laughed. "That's not a bear!" she said. She held a hand out to the creature. It came over, tongue hanging out. "It's a dog—a big dog."

"That's Seaman," a new voice said. "Are you children here to help us?"

MERIWETHER LEWIS BOUGHT SEAMAN FOR $20 IN PHILADELPHIA, PENNSYLVANIA. HE'S LISTED IN THE EXPEDITION RECORDS AS A "DOGG OF THE NEWFOUNDLAND BREED."

MERIWETHER LEWIS'S DOG, SEAMAN, WAS A MEMBER OF THE EXPEDITION. HE WAS A NEWFOUNDLAND. THIS BREED, OR KIND, OF DOG IS LARGE, STRONG, AND A GOOD SWIMMER.

The man looking at them was William Clark. The kids recognized him from a picture in their history book. After a moment, Ben spoke as Mia and Sam tried not to stare.

"Yes!" Ben said. "We'd like to go with you—if that's okay."

Clark paused. Then he nodded. "We set out at 4 o'clock," he told them. "That's very soon. You need to help, though. The men are loading the boats."

"Yes, sir!" Mia, Ben, and Sam said as they ran off, excited. Seaman ran with them.

LEWIS, CLARK, AND THEIR GROUP TRAVELED NEARLY 8,000 MILES (12,875 KM) ACROSS THE **CONTINENT** AND BACK. THIS MAP SHOWS THEIR **ROUTE** TO THE PACIFIC OCEAN AND THEIR RETURN.
MAP OF THE LEWIS AND CLARK EXPEDITION
FORT CLATSOP
BLACKFEET
GREAT FALLS
THREE FORKS
NEZ PERCÉ
SHOSHONE
COLUMBIA RIVER
SNAKE RIVER
FORT MANDAN
SIOUX
DEATH OF SGT. FLOYD
SAINT CHARLES
CAMP DUBOIS
ST. LOUIS
OHIO RIVER
PITTSBURGH
PHILADELPHIA
WASHINGTON, DC
SPANISH TERRITORY
LOUISIANA
ACQUIRED BY THE US IN 1803
UNITED STATES

CHAPTER 4: SETTING FORTH

There was one big boat called a keelboat and two smaller boats called pirogues (PEE-rohgz). The kids helped carry packages to the boats and store them. Then Clark arrived, and all the members of the expedition—including Mia, Ben, and Sam—climbed into the boats. One of the men fired a gun off the keelboat, making them jump.

A bunch of people who lived nearby came to see them off. Team Time Machine waved as the boat began to move. They were part of the Corps of Discovery!

THE KEELBOAT WAS REALLY BIG! IT WAS ABOUT 55 FEET (17 M) LONG AND 8 FEET (2.4 M) WIDE. THAT'S BIGGER THAN A SCHOOL BUS. IT COULD CARRY 10 TONS (9 MT) OF SUPPLIES.

THE EXPEDITION MOVED THE BOATS ABOUT 10 TO 20 MILES (16 TO 32 KM) A DAY. THEY ROWED, USED POLES, AND SOMETIMES PUSHED AND PULLED THEIR BOATS.

CHAPTER 5: MEN OF THE CORPS

Mia, Ben, and Sam made friends with the Corps of Discovery. Meriwether Lewis joined the group a few days later. He took lots of notes of all the places they passed. The kids liked watching him draw plants and animals.

John Ordway, a young soldier from New Hampshire, wrote in his journal a lot too. In fact, he did it every day of the journey—863 days! The other men were from many states, including Virginia, Kentucky, and Pennsylvania.

ANOTHER MAN IN THE CORPS OF DISCOVERY WAS NAMED YORK. HE WAS CALLED WILLIAM CLARK'S SERVANT, BUT HE WAS REALLY A SLAVE. YEARS AFTER THE TRIP, CLARK GAVE YORK HIS FREEDOM.

ONLY ONE MEMBER OF THE CORPS DIED DURING THE JOURNEY. CHARLES FLOYD DIED AUGUST 20, 1804, LIKELY FROM A BURST **APPENDIX**. THIS MONUMENT IN SIOUX CITY, IOWA, MARKS HIS GRAVE.

CHARLES FLOYD

CHAPTER 6: A VERY LONG TRIP

Weeks went went by. The trip was a lot of hard work. Many of the Corps were often sick, and they didn't have much **medicine** to help. The explorers slept in tents, but as time went on, the tents fell apart. (The Corps didn't have any left when they reached the coast!)

The kids missed modern food most of all. The expedition had brought food but counted on hunting and fishing a lot. They traded with Native Americans when supplies were low.

LEWIS, CLARK, AND THEIR TEAM SAW BISON ON THEIR JOURNEY THROUGH THE GREAT PLAINS. THE HUGE CREATURES PROVIDED MEAT FOR THE CORPS A NUMBER OF TIMES.

"I don't think we can tag along much longer," Sam admitted in October. "I love camping, but we've been traveling for months. The trip's not even halfway done!"

"I'd really like to meet Sacagawea, though!" Mia said. "I thought she was with the Corps the whole time."

Ben reminded her, "Lewis and Clark hire her husband Toussaint Charbonneau as an **interpreter** during the first winter of the journey, in North Dakota."

"That's right, and we're in North Dakota now. Let's keep going," Mia said.

SACAGAWEA WAS A SHOSHONE WOMAN WHO TRAVELED WITH THE CORPS OF DISCOVERY AS AN INTERPRETER. SHE HELPED THEM FIND THE BEST ROUTE WEST. SHE LATER APPEARED ON A U.S. DOLLAR COIN.

CHAPTER 7: MEETING SACAGAWEA

In a few days, the expedition reached Native American communities north of Bismarck, North Dakota. They saw people living in **lodges** made of earth and branches. Members of the Corps said these were the Mandan and Hidatsa villages.

"Yes!" Mia said excitedly, clapping her hands. "Sacagawea lives here!"

Lewis and Clark decided to build a fort across the Missouri River so they could stay the winter. They called it Fort Mandan "in honour of our neighbours," wrote Lewis. The kids helped build the cabins.

ABOUT 4,500 PEOPLE LIVED IN THE MANDAN AND HIDATSA VILLAGES. THAT'S MORE PEOPLE THAN LIVED IN ST. LOUIS, MISSOURI, AT THE TIME.

THIS LODGE IS A RE-CREATION OF THOSE THAT WOULD HAVE STOOD IN THE NATIVE AMERICAN VILLAGES WHERE SACAGAWEA MET LEWIS AND CLARK IN 1804.

Walking through the villages later, the kids saw Clark talking to a man near the river. Nearby, a young woman stood, looking away from them over the water.

Sam started to call out to Clark. He stopped, but the woman heard him. She looked over at them and smiled.

"Sacagawea!" Mia whispered. Then she saw the woman's round belly. "Oh! She's going to have a baby!"

"She has her baby in February," Ben told her. "He's only two months old when they start traveling."

THE HIDATSA TOOK SACAGAWEA FROM THE SHOSHONE WHEN SHE WAS ONLY 12. LEWIS AND CLARK HOPED SHE WOULD BE ABLE TO HELP THEM TALK TO OTHER SHOSHONE ON THE JOURNEY.

CHAPTER 8: WHAT HAPPENS NEXT?

By April 1805, the kids knew it was time to go home. There were adventures they'd miss, such as Sacagawea finding her brother. He had become a Shoshone chief. There were hardships, too. The men were often cold and hungry.

"I know the expedition never finds a water route all the way to the ocean," Ben said. "But they make it to the Pacific Ocean, right?"

Mia nodded. "It's a hard trip, but they find the Pacific."

THE CORPS OF DISCOVERY BUILT FORT CLATSOP NEAR TODAY'S ASTORIA, OREGON, AND SPENT THE WINTER OF 1805 THERE.

THE EXPEDITION MADE IT TO THE PACIFIC COAST BY MID-NOVEMBER 1805. WHEN CLARK FIRST SAW THE PACIFIC OCEAN, HE WROTE, "OCIAN IN VIEW! O! THE JOY."

RE-CREATION OF FORT CLATSOP

On April 7, 1805, most of the Corps of Discovery headed west. The kids and other expedition members headed east. They had maps, reports, and even a live prairie dog for Thomas Jefferson! When their boat neared the Team Time Machine library, the kids got off and said goodbye.

Sam sighed as he opened the door to the library. "I wish we could have completed the whole trip."

Ben and Mia laughed.

"I'm ready to sleep in a real bed," Ben said. "I've had enough camping for a long time!"

TODAY, YOU CAN TRACE LEWIS AND CLARK'S EXPEDITION THROUGH THE NATIONAL PARKS SERVICE. HAVE YOUR OWN EXPEDITION WITH YOUR FAMILY!
LEWIS AND CLARK TRAIL

appendix: a small part of the human body that can be removed if it becomes infected, or full of germs

continent: one of Earth's seven great landmasses

corps: a group of soldiers or people trained for special service

expedition: a trip made for a certain purpose

explorer: someone who travels to new places in order to find out new things

interpreter: someone who interprets, or tells the meaning of another language

lodge: a hut of Native Americans, usually having an arched frame of poles with bark, mats, or hides over it

medicine: a drug taken to make a sick person well

re-creation: something that was made again

route: a course that people travel

FOR MORE INFORMATION

BOOKS

Lawrence, Blythe. *The Lewis and Clark Expedition.* New York, NY: AV2 by Weigl, 2020.

Strand, Jennifer. *Lewis and Clark.* Minneapolis, MN: Abdo Zoom, 2017.

WEBSITES

America Heads West
kids.nationalgeographic.com/explore/history/lewis-and-clark/
This website gives more information about the expedition and where it fits in U.S. history.

The Lewis and Clark Expedition: Interactive Map
www.gilderlehrman.org/history-now/online-exhibitions/lewis-and-clark-expedition-interactive-map
Follow along on the journey with this interactive map showing Lewis and Clark's route.

What Was the Lewis and Clark Expedition?
www.wonderopolis.org/wonder/what-was-the-lewis-and-clark-expedition
Complete activities to help you understand more about the journey.

INDEX